TERRIBLE TROLLS

I0799226

FANTASY CREATURES

Gareth Stevens PUBLISHING

HOT TOPICS

BENJAMIN PROUDFIT

Please visit our website, www.garethstevens.com. For a free color catalog of all our high-quality books, call toll free 1-800-542-2595 or fax 1-877-542-2596.

Library of Congress Cataloging-in-Publication Data
Names: Proudfit, Benjamin.
Title: Terrible trolls / Benjamin Proudfit.
Description: Buffalo, NY : Gareth Stevens Publishing, 2026. | Series: Fantasy creatures | Includes glossary and index.
Identifiers: ISBN 9781482475364 (pbk.) | ISBN 9781482475371 (library bound) | ISBN 9781482475388 (ebook)
Subjects: LCSH: Food allergy in children–Juvenile literature.
Classification: LCC P93 2026 | DDC –dc23

Published in 2026 by
Gareth Stevens Publishing
2544 Clinton Street
Buffalo, NY 14224

Copyright © 2026 Gareth Stevens Publishing

Designer: Leslie Taylor
Editor: Kristen Nelson

Photo credits: Cover (troll) Shutterstock AI Generator/Shutterstock.com; cover and series art (neon circle) Ikrill/Shutterstock.com, (rough frame) TarnishArt/Shutterstock.com, (splotchy background) TiffanyShanks/Shutterstock.com; p. 10, 13, 23 Shutterstock AI Generator/Shuttertock.com; p. 5 quiggyt4/Shutterstock.com; p. 7 Tom Korcak/Shutterstock.com; p. 9 ztr_analog/Shutterstock.com; p. 11 Simbert Brause/Shutterstock.com; p. 15 David Pineda Svenske/Shutterstock.com; p. 17 Book authors Asbjornsen d. 1885 and Moe d. 1882/File:Asbjornsen and Moe's Norske folkeeventyr 1874 book cover.png_commons.wikimedia.org; p. 19 Dmitry Chulov/Shutterstock.com, (inset) Nicku/Shutterstock.com; p. 21 Barnabas Davoti/Shuttertstock.com, (self-portrait) National Museum of Art, Architecture and Design/File:Theodor Kittelsen - Self-Portrait - Google Art Project.jpg_commons.wikimedia.org, (drawing) Theodor Kittelsen/File:Theodor Kittelsen, Askeladden.jpg_commons.wikimedia.org; p. 25 Adam Constanza/Shutterstock.com; p. 27 (*Troll* poster) film poster for Troll/File:Troll (2022).jpeg_commons.wikimedia.org, (*Trollhunters* poster) poster for animated television series *Trollhunters*/File:Trollhunters poster.jpg_commons.wikimedia.org; p. 28 Suzanne Tucker/Shutterstock.com; p. 29 Faiz Zaki/Shutterstock.com; p. 30 (Trolltunga) fokke baarssen/Shutterstock.com, (Trollfjorden) Jelena Safronova/Shutterstock.com, (Trollkyrkja) Frank Fichtmueller/Shutterstock.com.

Some of the images in this book illustrate individuals who are models. The depictions do not imply actual situations or events.

All rights reserved. No part of this book may be reproduced in any form without permission in writing from the publisher, except by a reviewer.

Printed in China

CPSIA compliance information: Batch #QWGS26: For further information contact Gareth Stevens, at 1-800-542-2595.

Find us on

CONTENTS

Which Troll?

Are the trolls you imagine mean, ugly, and not-too-smart? Or, do you picture colorful, fun little trolls? In the long history of troll stories, these fantasy creatures have been both!

IMAGINE THAT!

"FANTASY" IS A GENRE, OR GROUPING, OF BOOKS, MOVIES, AND SHOWS THAT HAVE TO DO WITH IMAGINATIVE STORIES THAT FEATURE IMPOSSIBLE EVENTS AND CHARACTERS.

Early Tales

Trolls are creatures from the **myths** of Scandinavia, or the northern European countries of Sweden, Norway, Denmark, and Iceland. Some of the first recorded troll stories come from around the year 1200. But these tales have been around for far longer.

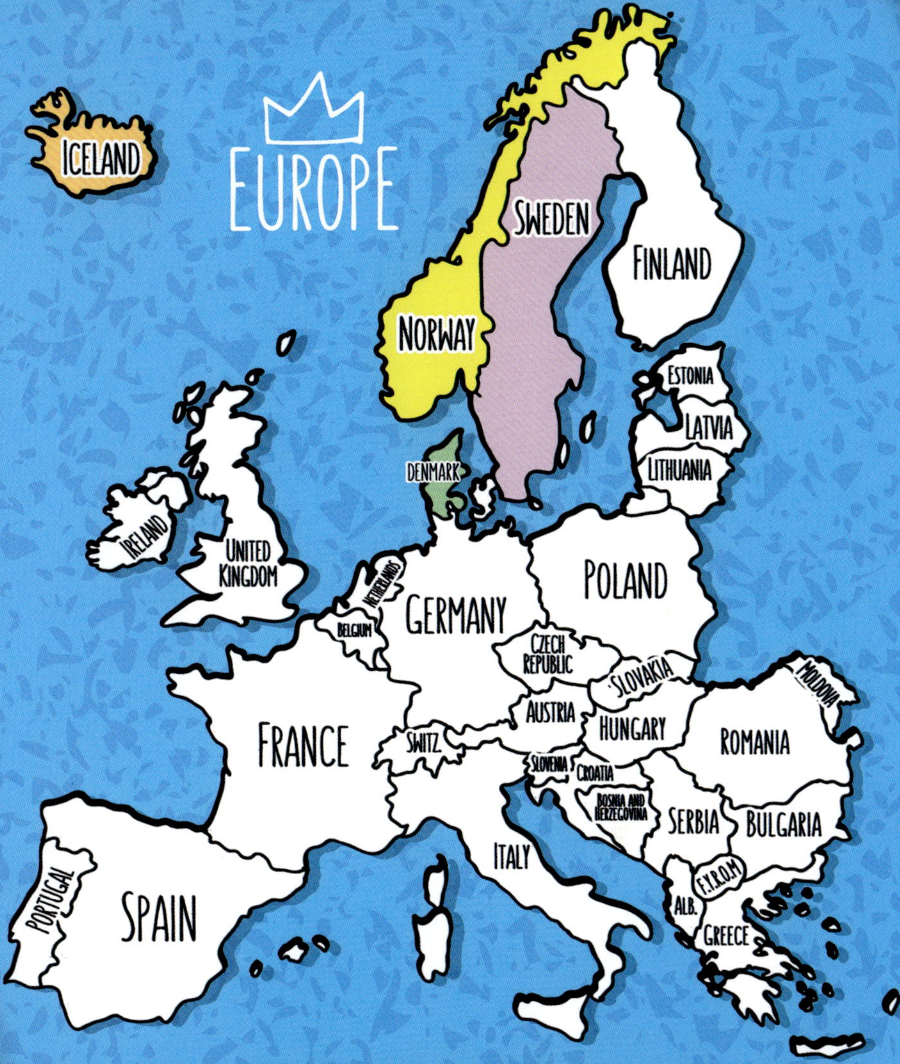

IMAGINE THAT!

THE MYTHS OF MANY **CULTURES**, INCLUDING THE TROLL STORIES OF SCANDINAVIA, WERE PASSED DOWN **ORALLY** BEFORE THEY WERE WRITTEN DOWN.

Some trolls in Scandinavian myths are said to be big as a mountain and evil. Others aren't very large and like to play tricks. Most trolls have one head, but some have three. They may have only one eye. There's one feature they all share though: They're ugly!

IMAGINE THAT!

SOME TROLLS STEAL CHILDREN IN STORIES.

Mountain Trolls

Myths divide trolls into two main kinds: mountain trolls and cave trolls. Mountain, or forest, trolls look a bit like huge, ugly humans with big noses. They aren't very smart but have a lot of strength. They can pull up trees by their roots!

IMAGINE THAT!

THE CARD GAME MAGIC THE GATHERING HAS MANY TROLL CARDS IN IT.

"The Three Billy Goats Gruff" comes from a Scandinavian tale featuring a mountain troll. The troll lives under a bridge and tries to stop goats from crossing. The small goats trick the troll into waiting for the biggest goat—who kills the troll!

IMAGINE THAT!

IN FOLKTALES, THE WAY TO BEAT A MOUNTAIN TROLL IS BY TRICKING OR OUTSMARTING IT.

Cave Trolls

Cave trolls are smaller than mountain trolls. They have round bellies and are said to be especially ugly. These trolls live underground and in caves. Stories say they try to play mean tricks on humans.

IMAGINE THAT!

MYTHS SAY TROLLS CAN'T GO OUT INTO THE SUN. IT TURNS THEM INTO STONE!

In the 1800s

During the 1800s, Peter Christen Asbjørnsen and Jørgen Moe collected stories about trolls from the countryside of Norway. They published, or put out, their **versions** in a book of folktales. Their versions became very popular and shaped how troll stories are known today.

IMAGINE THAT!

TROLL STORIES WERE LIKELY TOLD BECAUSE EARLY PEOPLE COULDN'T ALWAYS EXPLAIN THE WORLD AROUND THEM.

BOOK OF NORWEGIAN FOLKTALES

Norwegian writer Henrik Ibsen had trolls in his 1867 play *Peer Gynt*. The play tells of the troll king Dovregubben. Composer Edvard Grieg wrote music to go with this play. His most famous piece came from this work: "I Dovregubbens hall (In The Hall of the Mountain King)."

IMAGINE THAT!

IN THE PLAY, DOVREGUBBEN SYMBOLIZES, OR STANDS FOR, PEOPLE WHO DO NOT EASILY **ACCEPT** IDEAS THAT ARE DIFFERENT FROM THEIR OWN.

HENRIK IBSEN

EDVARD GRIEG

Nothing has shaped the look of trolls today more than the artwork of Theodor Kittelsen. In the 1880s, his work was part of a new **edition** of folktales by Asbjørnsen and Moe. Kittelsen's art shows trolls as a bit scary, but also beautiful in a way.

IMAGINE THAT!

ANOTHER ARTIST TOLD ASBJØRNSEN AND MOE TO HIRE KITTELSEN BECAUSE KITTELSEN WAS GOOD AT PAINTING "WHAT IS NOT REAL."

SCULPTURE OF THEODOR KITTELSEN

KITTELSEN'S ARTWORK

KITTELSEN'S SELF-PORTRAIT

Thirteen Lads

Over time, some troll tales have come to show trolls as kinder creatures. Today in Iceland, the Yule Lads are 13 brothers who bring gifts to children for 13 days before Christmas. This comes from an old folktale about trolls and their mother who might eat **naughty** children!

IMAGINE THAT!

PARENTS USED THIS TROLL STORY TO SCARE CHILDREN INTO **BEHAVING**. KIDS WERE SO SCARED, IN 1746, THE GOVERNMENT OF ICELAND OUTLAWED TELLING THESE STORIES TO GET CHILDREN TO BEHAVE.

Trolls in Pop Culture

The trolls featured in *The Lord of the Rings* and *Harry Potter* series are based on mountain trolls. They're mean and ugly! The look of the trolls in the *Frozen* movies are based more on cave trolls. But, in *Frozen*, the trolls are helpful and smart!

IMAGINE THAT!

IN *THE LORD OF THE RINGS* BOOKS AND MOVIES, TROLLS ARE ALWAYS ON THE SIDE OF EVIL.

Two Norwegian-made movies have brought more **traditional** ideas about trolls to the world. The look of the trolls in the 2010 movie *Troll Hunter* even seem to be based on Kittelsen's pictures. *Troll,* which came out in 2022, broke records when it came out on Netflix.

IMAGINE THAT!

THE **ANIMATED** SHOW *TROLLHUNTERS* IS MADE FOR KIDS. IT FOLLOWS A BOY WHO MEETS TROLLS AND WORKS TO KEEP THEM SAFE.

MOUNTAINS WILL MOVE
A NETFLIX FILM
TROLL
DECEMBER 1 | NETFLIX

A NETFLIX ORIGINAL SERIES
DREAMWORKS
TROLLHUNTERS
GUILLERMO DEL TORO
ALL EPISODES
DECEMBER 23 | NETFLIX

Trolls ... That Sing!

In 2016, a movie about colorful trolls that sing, dance, and hug hit the big screen. *Trolls* introduced a whole new group of children to this fantasy creature. Poppy, Branch, and their friends were friendly, kind, and cute!

IMAGINE THAT!

THE THREE *TROLLS* MOVIES WERE BASED ON TROLL DOLLS, WHICH HAVE BEEN POPULAR AT DIFFERENT TIMES OVER THE YEARS. THEY WERE FIRST MADE IN DENMARK IN THE 1950S.

Go Troll Hunting!

Do you want to find a troll—or at least see some beautiful nature? These places in Norway are named for trolls!

TROLLSTIGEN

"the troll ladder," a winding road up a hillside

TROLLVEGGEN

"the troll wall" is the highest drop in all of Europe

TROLLTUNGA

hike up 3,800 feet (1,158 m) to see a great view

TROLLFJORDEN

"the troll fjord" found in northern Norway

TROLLKIRKA

caves, underground rivers, and waterfalls

FOR MORE INFORMATION

BOOKS

Munsey, Lizzie, et al. *Supernatural Creatures: Mythical and Sacred Creatures from Around the World.* New York, NY: DK, 2024.

Nardo, Don. *Creatures and Beasts in World Mythology.* San Diego, CA: ReferencePoint Press, Inc., 2025.

WEBSITES

Fantasy Books for Kids
https://www.commonsensemedia.org/lists/fantasy-books-for-kids
Find lots of great fantasy books for kids here.

Fantasy Movies for Kids
https://www.commonsensemedia.org/lists/best-fantasy-movies
Find your next favorite fantasy movie here!

Publisher's note to educators and parents: Our editors have carefully reviewed these websites to ensure that they are suitable for students. Many websites change frequently, however, and we cannot guarantee that a site's future contents will continue to meet our high standards of quality and educational value. Be advised that students should be closely supervised whenever they access the internet.

GLOSSARY

accept: To receive something willingly.

animated: Consisting of drawings or computer images that appear to move.

behave: To act in the right way.

culture: The beliefs and ways of life of a group of people.

edition: The form in which something is published.

myth: Story that was told by a people to explain a practice, belief, or natural event.

naughty: Poorly behaved.

oral: Spoken.

version: A form of something that is different from others.

traditional: Having to do with long-practiced customs.

INDEX